D0927010

GRAPHIC MODERN HISTORY: WORLD WAR II

WAR IN THE PACIFIC

By Gary Jeffrey & Illustrated by Nick Spender

Crabtree Publishing Company
www.crabtreebooks.com

Crabtree Publishing Company

www.crabtreebooks.com

Created and produced by:
David West Children's Books

Project development, design, and concept:
David West Children's Books

Author and designer: Gary Jeffrey

Illustrator: Nick Spender

Editor: Lynn Peppas

Proofreader: Wendy Scavuzzo

Project coordinator: Kathy Middleton

Production and print coordinator:
Katherine Berti

Prepress technician: Katherine Berti

Photographs:
National Archives: page 4b U.S.Navy:
page 5b US Army Air Forces: page 44bl
Army Signal Corps: page 45br Staff
Sergent Walter F. Kleine: page 47b

Library and Archives Canada Cataloguing in Publication

Jeffrey, Gary
War in the Pacific / Gary Jeffrey ; illustrated by Nick Spender.

(Graphic modern history World War II)
Includes index.
Issued also in electronic formats.
ISBN 978-0-7787-4197-8 (bound).--ISBN 978-0-7787-4204-3 (pbk.)

1. World War, 1939-1945--Campaigns--Pacific Area--Comic books, strips, etc. 2. World War, 1939-1945--Campaigns--Pacific Area--Juvenile literature. 3. Graphic novels. I. Spender, Nik II. Title. III. Series: Jeffrey, Gary. Graphic modern history World War II.

D767.J44 2012   j940.54'26   C2011-908348-5

Library of Congress Cataloging-in-Publication Data

Jeffrey, Gary.
War in the Pacific / Gary Jeffrey ; illustrated by Nick Spender.
p. cm. -- (Graphic modern history. World War II)
Includes index.
ISBN 978-0-7787-4197-8 (reinforced library binding : alk. paper) -- ISBN 978-0-7787-4204-3 (pbk. : alk. paper) -- ISBN 978-1-4271-7877-0 (electronic pdf) -- ISBN 978-1-4271-7992-0 (electronic html)
1. World War, 1939-1945--Campaigns--Pacific Area--Comic books, strips, etc. 2. World War, 1939-1945--Campaigns--Pacific Area--Juvenile literature. 3. Graphic novels. I. Spender, Nik. II. Title.

D767.J44 2012
940.54'26--dc23

2011050084

Crabtree Publishing Company

www.crabtreebooks.com   1-800-387-7650

Printed in the U.S.A./062013/SP20130610

Published in Canada
Crabtree Publishing
616 Welland Ave.
St. Catharines, Ontario
L2M 5V6

Published in the United States
Crabtree Publishing
PMB 59051
350 Fifth Avenue, 59th Floor
New York, New York 10118

Published in the United Kingdom
Crabtree Publishing
Maritime House
Basin Road North, Hove
BN41 1WR

Published in Australia
Crabtree Publishing
3 Charles Street
Coburg North
VIC 3058

CONTENTS

THE PACIFIC CONQUERED   4

TURNING THE TIDE   6

GEORGE H. GAY, JR.
TORPEDO RUN—
THE BATTLE OF MIDWAY
JUNE 4, 1942   8

JAMES J. FAHEY
KAMIKAZE ATTACK!—
LEYTE GULF
NOVEMBER 27, 1944   20

MARION "FRANK" WALKER
CAPTURING MOUNT
SURIBACHI—THE BATTLE
OF IWO JIMA
FEBRUARY 19, 1945   32

ULTIMATE FORCE   44

GLOSSARY   46

INDEX   48

THE PACIFIC CONQUERE**I**

In 1940, the Japanese signed an agreement with Germany and fascist Italy. If either one of them was attacked by the United States, the other would help. After expanding their empire by invading part of China in 1937, the Japanese were now free to fulfill what they believed was their ultimate destiny—to rule all of East Asia.

DAY OF INFAMY

During 1941, the United States' policy was to aid the Allies, but otherwise stay out of the war in Europe. In the Pacific, they forced sanctions on Japan to deny them oil and the other raw materials they needed for their expansion. To get what they needed, Japan would have to challenge the United States.

The attack, as seen from a Japanese bomber. Luckily, fuel storage areas remained untouched.

On December 7, 1941, they launched an attack on the US Naval base at Pearl Harbor, Hawaii. It was a complete surprise. Losing 29 aircraft, the Japanese destroyed seven ships (including four battleships) and damaged 10 more. More than 340 US aircraft were destroyed or damaged, and 3,600 people were killed or wounded. The US aircraft carriers were spared because they were all out at sea. Speaking to the nation, President Roosevelt described it as *"...a day of infamy."*

On December 8, the United States declared war on Japan. Three days later, Germany declared war on the United States. The United States in turn declared war on Germany. The Japanese hoped they had damaged the US Navy badly enough to give them a chance of winning.

USS Arizona sank, resulting in the loss of 1,177 lives.

INVADERS

While the United States recalled its carriers and began repairs at Pearl Harbor, the Japanese quickly invaded Guam and Wake Island. During the first five months of 1942, Japan successfully neutralized the standing Allied Pacific fleet and invaded the Philippines, the Dutch East Indies (Indonesia), Hong Kong, Singapore, Malaya, and Burma.

With no battleships ready, all the United States could do was defend their home territory—a line that stretched from Hawaii to Midway Atoll (with supply lines running to Australia), and make a small number of carrier-based raids.

By April, the Japanese had taken the Northern Soloman Islands and had an invasion force ready to land in the south of New Guinea. They intended to cut Australia's supply lines and launch air attacks on the colony.

The victorious Japanese march into Singapore, the premier city of British Malaya, in February 1942.

On April 18, a daring American air raid was made against Tokyo from carriers in the Pacific. Although little damage was done, the Doolittle Raid shocked the Japanese into committing ships to defend its home waters.

STANDOFF

The United States quickly sent out the only carriers they had ready, *Yorktown* and *Lexington*, and five destroyers to intercept the Japanese in the Coral Sea. The Japanese force was two large carriers, two heavy cruisers, and two destroyers. The rest of the fleet was being mobilized for a planned attack on Midway. The result of the world's first major carrier battle (May 4–8, 1942) was a draw. Although the United States lost *Lexington*, Japan lost more planes and had to call off its assault on Australia.

Meanwhile, the Japanese had gathered all their spare forces for a massive attack on the air base at Midway. Their plan was to draw the US carriers out of Pearl Harbor and annihilate them. If they could beat the American ships out of the Pacific, they could negotiate a truce, and get on with conquering China.

The USS Lexington *burns in the Battle of the Coral Sea.*

TURNING THE TIDE

In May 1942, Admiral Yamamoto on his flagship *Yamoto*, the largest battleship in the world, led a combined fleet including six carriers and 10 battleships, east toward Hawaii. The Americans knew they were coming, and they knew they were vastly outnumbered, but they had one great ace up their sleeve—they had broken the Japanese Navy's code.

TURNING POINT

The code breakers that had enabled the Americans to surprise the Japanese in the Coral Sea, now identified, with as much certainty as was possible, that Midway was the combined fleet's target. They also gave Admiral Chester Nimitz, the US Navy's supreme commander, a complete list of all the Japanese ships and what their approximate positions would be.

By taking out three enemy carriers in just under six minutes on June 4, US Navy dive bombers turned the tide at Midway.

Nimitz decided to gamble on the intelligence. He stationed his fleet of three carriers just off Midway, and packed the island with bombers and anti-aircraft guns. They would wait for the Japanese to strike, then ambush them. The Battle of Midway (June 4–7, 1942) was a decisive victory for the Allies. The Japanese suffered four carriers sunk and, more importantly, lost many of their veteran pilots. The United States lost the USS *Yorktown* but had tipped the balance of power in the Pacific. They were now on the offensive.

Guadalcanal proved to be a trial by fire for US forces.

GUADALCANAL

In August 1942, 11,000 US ground troops landed on Guadalcanal in the Soloman Islands to stop the Japanese from building an air base. The land and naval battles of Guadalcanal (August 7, 1942 to February 9, 1943) became the stubborn resistance of Allied forces against unrelenting Japanese attempts to retake the island, forcing the Japanese to eventually give up.

THE BATTLE FOR THE MARIANAS AND THE PHILIPPINES

During most of 1943, the United States and Japan focused mainly on building up their navies and, by mid-1944, the United States had built five large carriers and eight battleships to add to its fleet. Beyond the central Pacific islands, the Allies' next big target was the Marianas—Saipan, Tinian, and Guam, which were needed to provide air bases from which to attack Japan.

Between 1942 and 1945, a British India "Special Force" of Chindits, was put deep into Japanese-occupied Burma. Along with Chinese and Indian forces, they eventually beat the Japanese back.

The resulting Battle of the Philippine Sea (June 19–20, 1944) turned into a disastrous carrier battle for the Japanese that wiped out most of their newly-trained pilots.

After Leyte Gulf, the Japanese relied on kamikaze, or suicide pilots, to counter the threat of the Allied navy.

The battle for the Philippines—The Battle of Leyte Gulf (October 23–26, 1944)—proved even worse. The largest naval battle of World War II saw the Japanese fleet decimated. The Americans finally won command of the sea. Only the Japanese homeland remained a stronghold.

INVADING JAPAN

The push was on to end the war. Since 1942, the United States had been working on a top secret doomsday weapon, but only as a method of last resort.

In 1945, plans went ahead to invade the outlying Japanese islands of Iwo Jima and Okinawa before a full-scale invasion of the Japanese home islands. Surrounded, and short of weapons, equipment, and fuel, the Japanese steeled themselves for a defiant resistance to the invaders.

Japanese Emperor Hirohito encouraged his people to commit mass suicide rather than surrender to the Allies.

George H. Gay, Jr. TORPEDO RUN—THE BATTLE OF MIDWAY JUNE 4, 1942

AT 0950 HOURS

THE 15 DOUGLAS DEVASTATOR TORPEDO BOMBERS FLEW BEHIND EACH OTHER IN A SCOUTING LINE.

THE BASE ON MIDWAY ATOLL HAD BEEN HIT BY JAPANESE BOMBERS JUST HOURS EARLIER.

SQUADRON 8 HAD BEEN LAUNCHED FROM USS HORNET - PART OF A WAVE OF AIRCRAFT OUT HUNTING FOR THE ENEMY CARRIERS.

LIEUTENANT COMMANDER WALDRON'S VOICE CRACKLED OVER ENSIGN GEORGE GAY'S HEADSET...

I SEE SMOKE AND WAKES...

...WE'VE GOT THEM!

GAY COULD SEE AIRCRAFT GLITTERING ON THE CARRIER DECKS.

THEY MUST BE REFUELING THEIR BOMBERS FOR ANOTHER ATTACK.

WALDRON WAS RADIOING A CONTACT REPORT WHEN...

BANDITS! BANDITS! TWELVE O'CLOCK HIGH!

THE ZEROS CAME IN OUT OF THE SUN.

THE LUMBERING DEVASTATORS WERE EASY PREY FOR THE FAST, WELL-ARMED JAPANESE FIGHTERS.

AAAAGH!

I'M HIT! I'M HIT!

SQUADRON FORM UP! FORM UP!

IT WAS CARNAGE IN MID-AIR...

THE SURVIVORS REGROUPED INTO TIGHT FORMATION TO BEGIN THEIR ATTACK RUN.

GAY'S REAR GUNNER TRIED TO LAY COVERING FIRE AS THE ZEROS CAME IN AGAIN.

THEY'RE COMING IN TOO FAST!

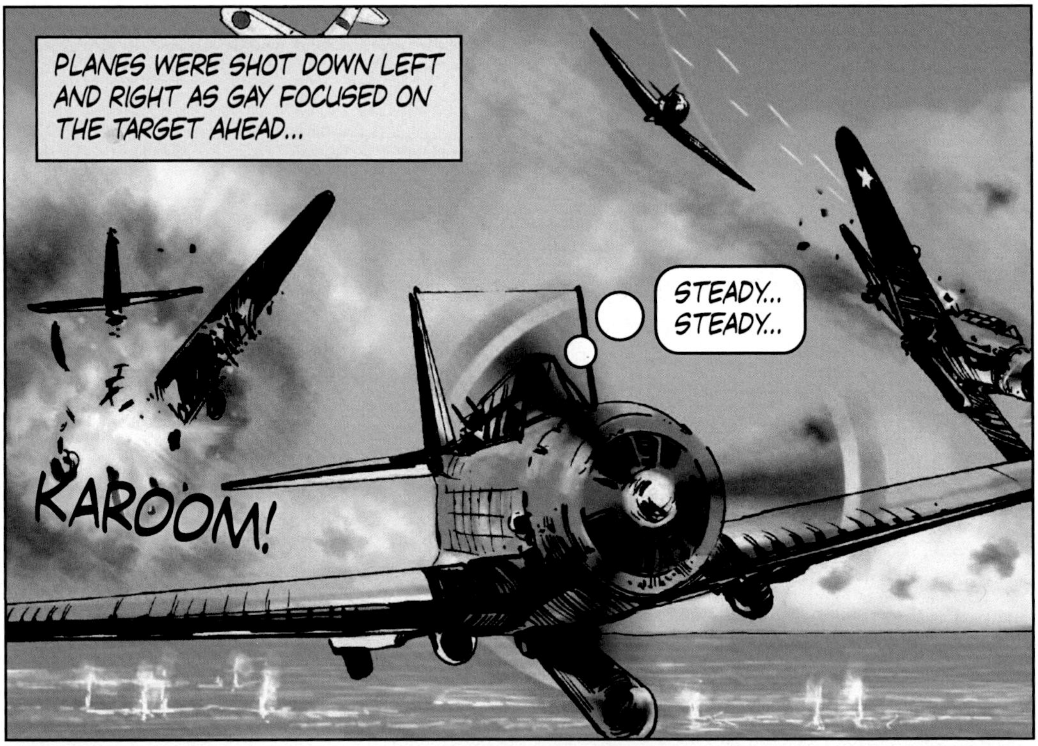
PLANES WERE SHOT DOWN LEFT AND RIGHT AS GAY FOCUSED ON THE TARGET AHEAD...
STEADY... STEADY...
KAROOM!

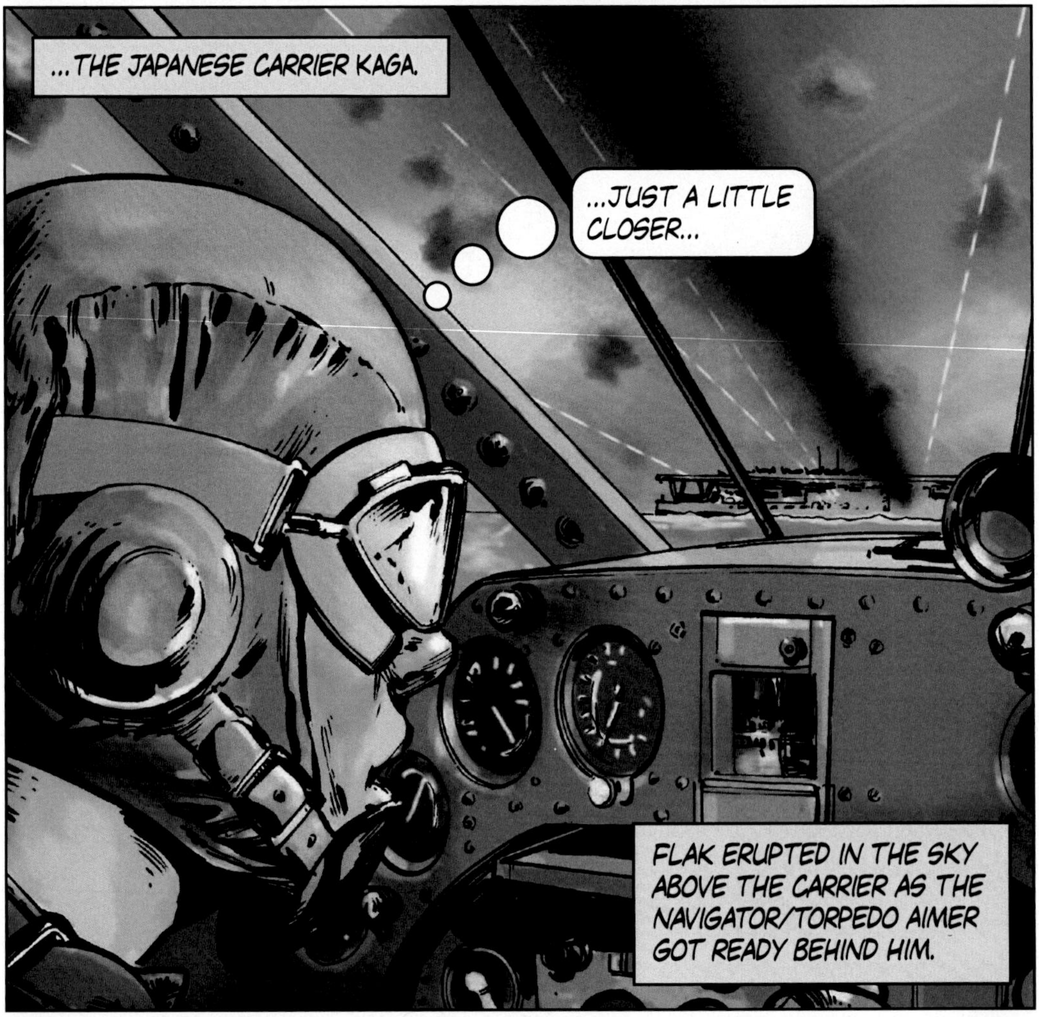
...THE JAPANESE CARRIER KAGA.
...JUST A LITTLE CLOSER...
FLAK ERUPTED IN THE SKY ABOVE THE CARRIER AS THE NAVIGATOR/TORPEDO AIMER GOT READY BEHIND HIM.

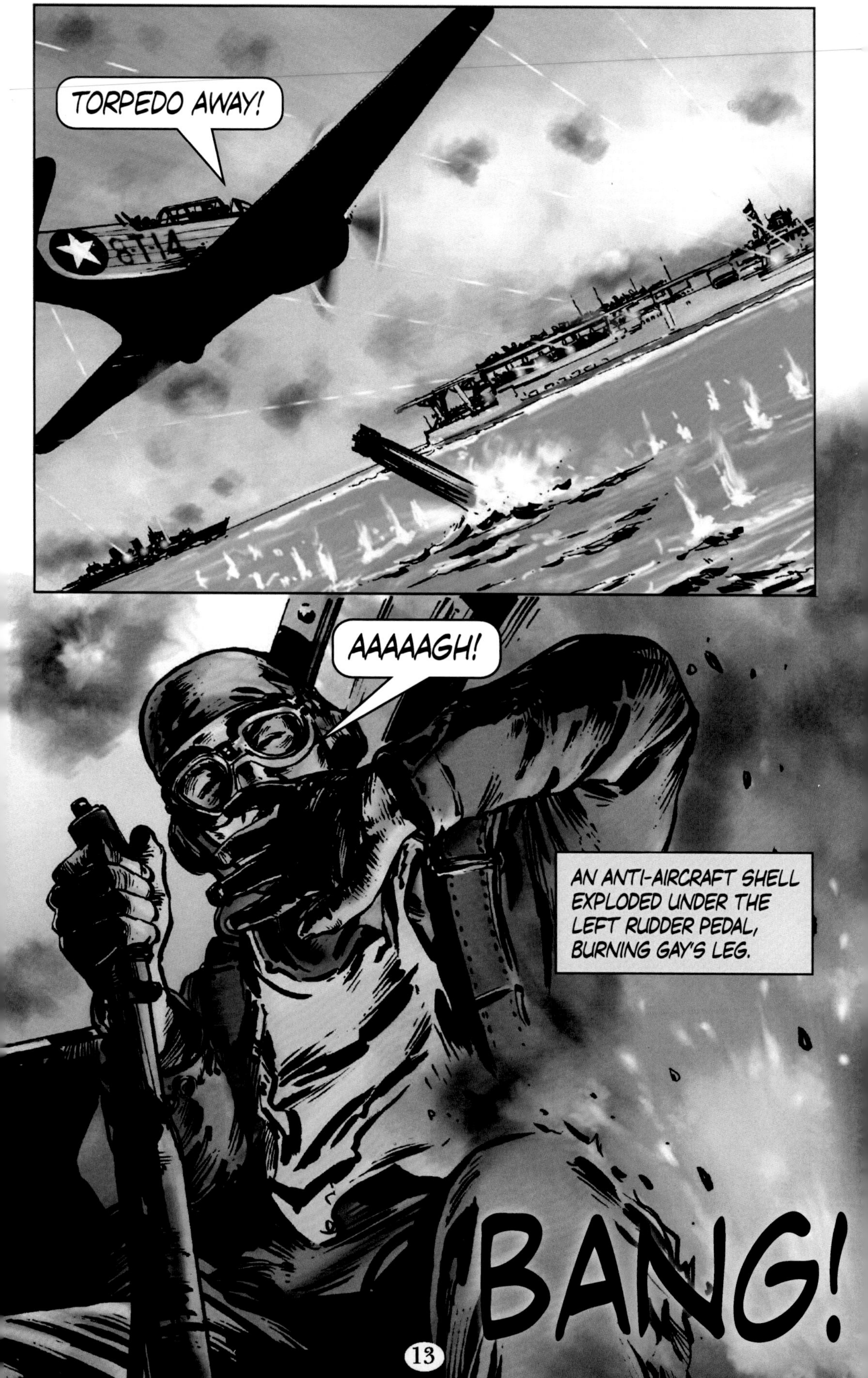
TORPEDO AWAY!
AAAAAGH!
AN ANTI-AIRCRAFT SHELL EXPLODED UNDER THE LEFT RUDDER PEDAL, BURNING GAY'S LEG.
BANG!

GAY CONTINUED TO FLY STRAIGHT AT THE KAGA, BANKING AT THE LAST MINUTE TO AVOID ITS BRIDGE TOWER.

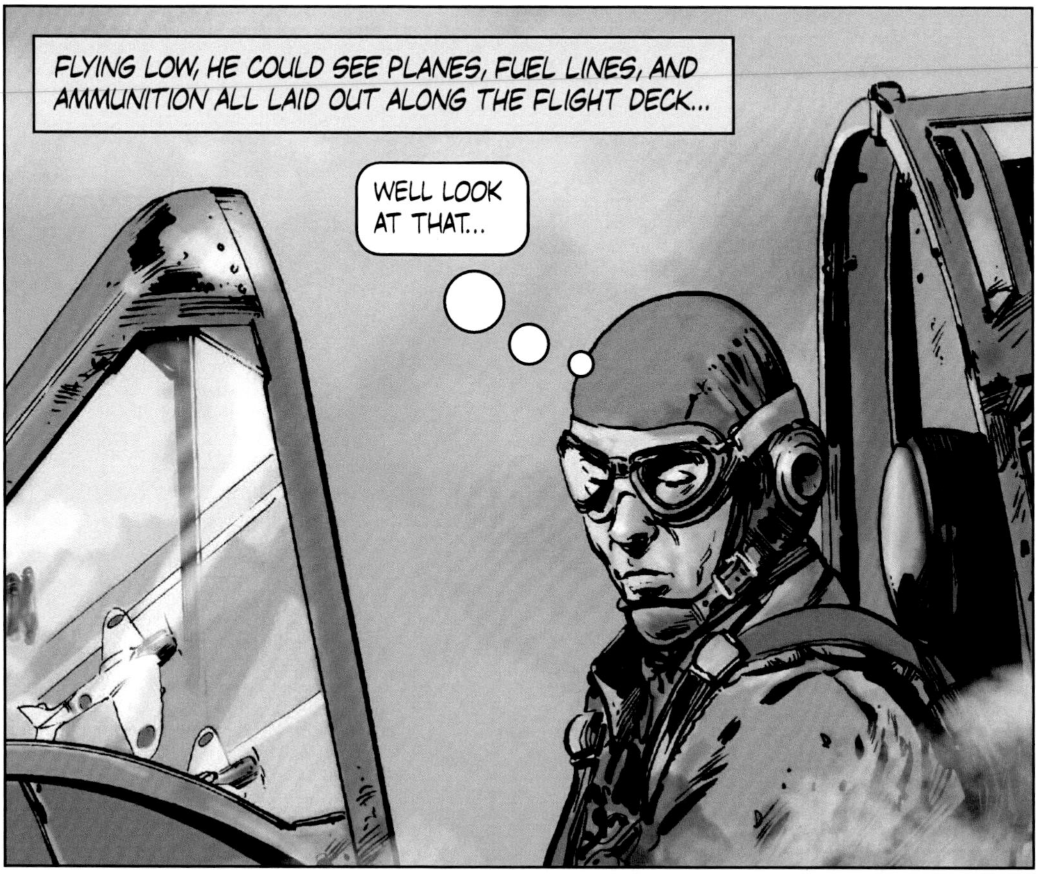
FLYING LOW, HE COULD SEE PLANES, FUEL LINES, AND AMMUNITION ALL LAID OUT ALONG THE FLIGHT DECK...
WELL LOOK AT THAT...

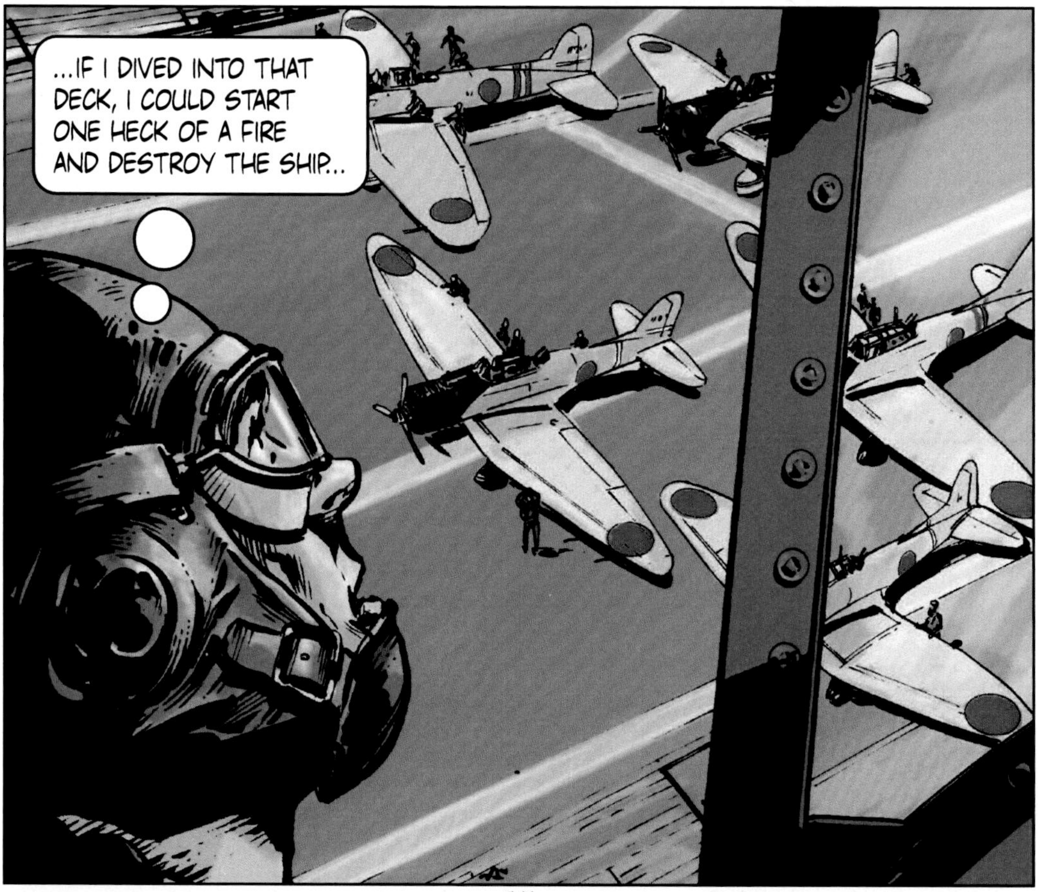
...IF I DIVED INTO THAT DECK, I COULD START ONE HECK OF A FIRE AND DESTROY THE SHIP...

BUT GAY DECIDED TO TRY TO RUN FOR HOME, HOTLY PURSUED BY ZEROS.

THE ZEROS LINED UP TO TAKE SHOTS AT THE SLOW-MOVING TORPEDO PLANE.

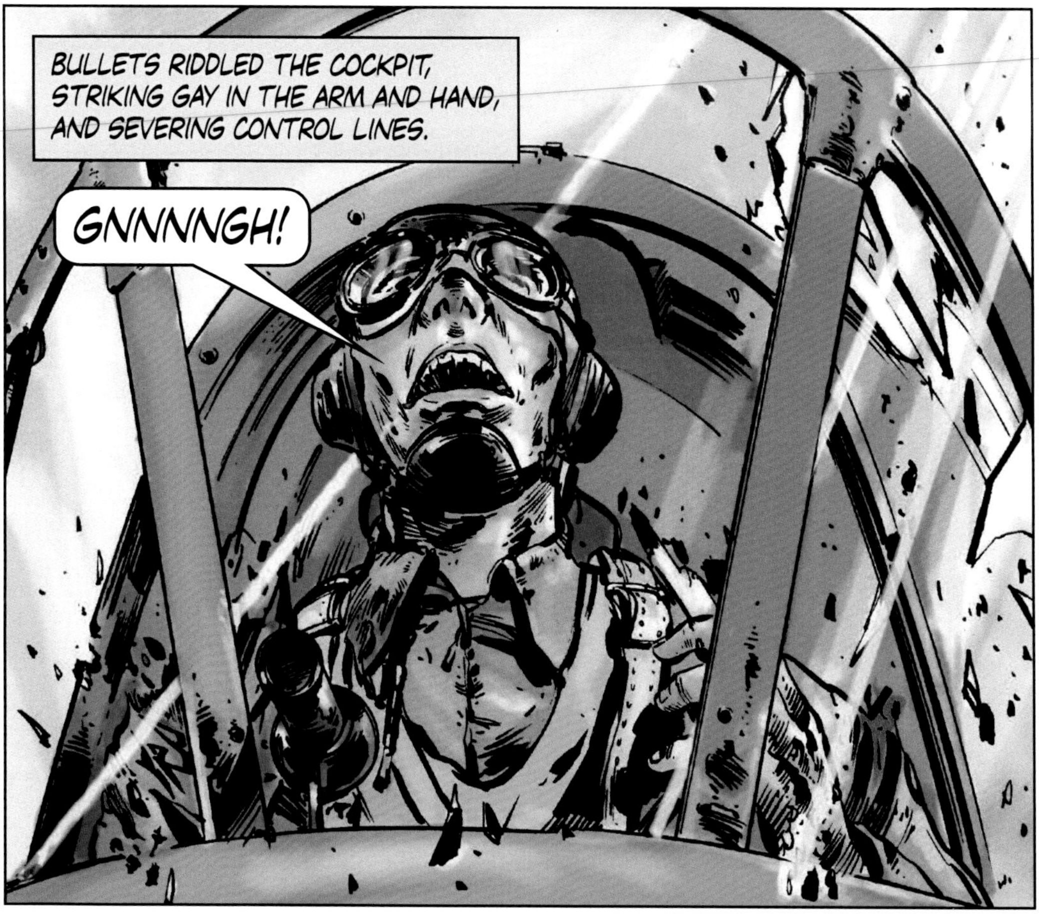
BULLETS RIDDLED THE COCKPIT, STRIKING GAY IN THE ARM AND HAND, AND SEVERING CONTROL LINES.
GNNNNGH!

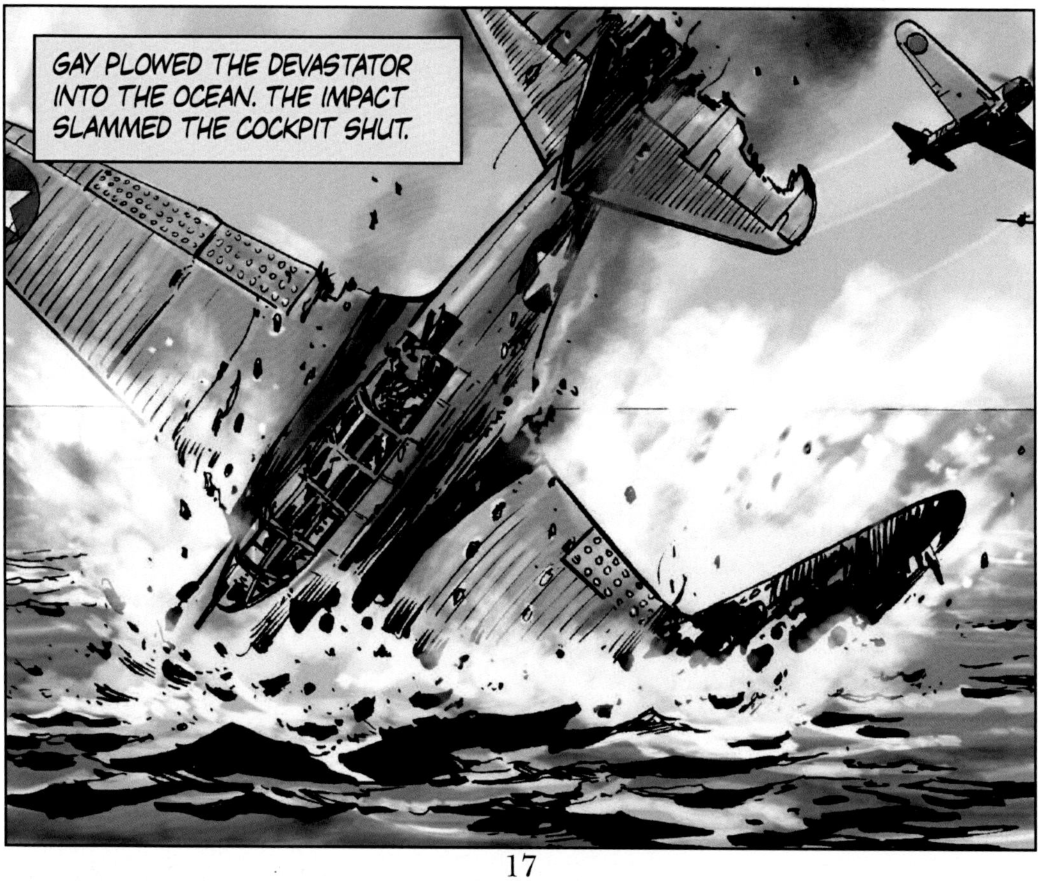
GAY PLOWED THE DEVASTATOR INTO THE OCEAN. THE IMPACT SLAMMED THE COCKPIT SHUT.

WITH GREAT EFFORT, GAY BROKE FREE OF THE SINKING PLANE. BUT THE NAVIGATOR AND REAR GUNNER WERE TRAPPED.

A JAPANESE DESTROYER CAME NEAR...

...AND GAY HID UNDERNEATH A FLOATING SEAT CUSHION UNTIL IT HAD PASSED.

AS THE DAY WORE ON, HE FOUND HIMSELF WITH A RINGSIDE SEAT AS WAVES OF AMERICAN DIVE BOMBERS ATTACKED THE JAPANESE FLEET, SINKING FOUR CARRIERS, ONE DESTROYER, AND HUNDREDS OF AIRCRAFT.

YEAH! GIVE IT TO 'EM!

GAY, THE SOLE SURVIVOR OF HIS 30-MAN SQUADRON, WAS RESCUED THE NEXT MORNING. HE WAS AWARDED THE NAVY CROSS, A PURPLE HEART, AND A PRESIDENTIAL UNIT CITATION FOR HIS ACTIONS AT MIDWAY.

THE END

JAMES J. FAHEY
KAMIKAZE ATTACK!—LEYTE GULF
NOVEMBER 27, 1944

AT LEYTE GULF, EAST OF THE PHILIPPINES, AT 1050 HOURS, A JAPANESE BOMBER PLOWED INTO THE WATER CLOSE TO A BATTLESHIP THAT WAS REFUELING FROM A TANKER.

ON THE NEARBY LIGHT CRUISER, USS MONTPELIER, FIRST CLASS SEAMAN JAMES FAHEY SAW IT HIT.

THAT WAS TOO CLOSE FOR COMFORT!

A BLARING ALARM CALLED "GENERAL QUARTERS" WAS SOUNDING. AN AIR RAID WAS IN PROGRESS.

ONE OF OUR P-38S MUST HAVE GOTTEN THE PILOT!

FAHEY TOOK HIS PLACE AS A LOADER ON THE STARBOARD GUN MOUNT.

THE REFUELING BATTLESHIP AND FAHEY'S CRUISER MOVED TO REJOIN THE REST OF THE TASK FORCE AS THEY CIRCLED DEFENSIVELY AROUND THE TANKER.

ENEMY BOMBERS DROPPED OUT OF THE CLOUDS.

BOOM!
BOOM!
BOOM!
BOOM

THEY CAME AT THE SHIPS FROM
EVERY DIRECTION. FAHEY SWUNG
HIS GUN MOUNT LEFT AND RIGHT,
RAPID-FIRING EXPLOSIVE SHELLS.

CLINK!
CLINK!

CLINK!

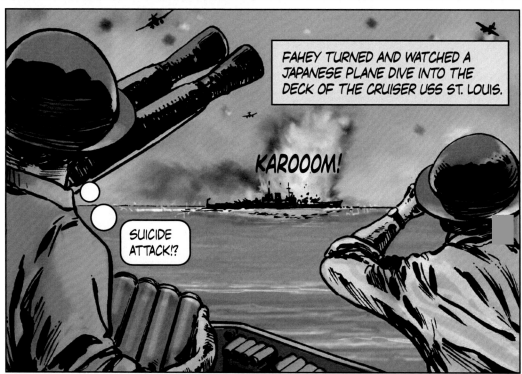

FAHEY TURNED AND WATCHED A
JAPANESE PLANE DIVE INTO THE
DECK OF THE CRUISER USS ST. LOUIS.

KAROOOM!

SUICIDE
ATTACK!?

WHILE THEY TRAINED THEIR GUNS ON AN INCOMING PLANE, ANOTHER JAPANESE PILOT MADE A BEELINE FOR FAHEY'S POSITION.

LUCKILY, THE PORT GUNNERS SWUNG AROUND AND TOOK ITS WING OFF.

BANG!

AS IT HIT THE WATER, ITS BOMB EXPLODED, SHOWERING THE STERN WITH DEBRIS.

THAT WAS TOO CLOSE!

KAROOM!

THINGS WOULD GET EVEN CLOSER AS A PLANE SLAMMED INTO THE GUN TURRET BELOW FAHEY, BUCKLING IT. HE WATCHED AS SAILORS RACED TO TOSS LIVE SHELLS OVER THE SIDE.

IF THE FIRE GETS THEM, THE SHIP IS GONE.

FAHEY GLANCED UP TO SEE A PLANE MAKING A STEEP CLIMB INTO THE AIR ABOVE THE SHIPS.

THE PILOT WAS MANEUVERING TO TURN...

...AND MAKE A DIVE STRAIGHT DOWN...

...ONTO THE DECK OF THE MONTPELIER.

NOW IS NOT THE TIME TO RUN OUT OF AMMUNITION!

GET HIM!

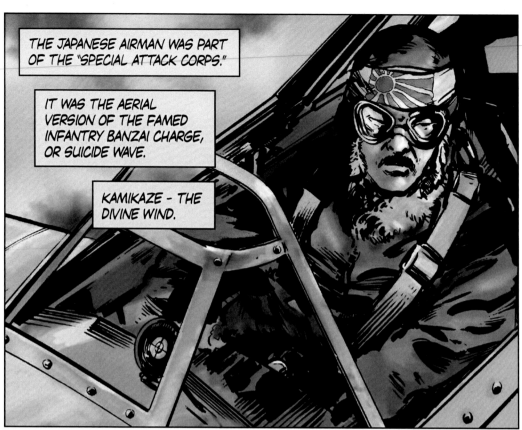

THE JAPANESE AIRMAN WAS PART OF THE "SPECIAL ATTACK CORPS."

IT WAS THE AERIAL VERSION OF THE FAMED INFANTRY BANZAI CHARGE, OR SUICIDE WAVE.

KAMIKAZE - THE DIVINE WIND.

AT THE MOMENT OF IMPACT, THE PILOTS WERE TO SHOUT...

...HISSATU!

IT MEANT "SINK WITHOUT FAIL."

THE PLANE JUST MISSED FAHEY AND LANDED IN THE OCEAN.

PLANE PARTS AND WATER RAINED DOWN ON THE GUN CREW.

UNNNGH!

FOR TWO LONG HOURS, THE
SHIPS FENDED OFF WAVE AFTER
WAVE OF KAMIKAZE ATTACKS.

DEBRIS RAINED DOWN FROM THE SKY.

THERE WERE MANY CASUALTIES. FAHEY SAW HIS BEST BUDDY, TOMLINSON, STRETCHERED TO THE INFIRMARY AFTER HE WAS HIT BY A BIG PIECE OF AIRCRAFT ENGINE.

AT LAST THE BATTLE WAS OVER...

...AND AT LEAST THE PRECIOUS TANKER HAS BEEN SAVED.

NEXT CAME THE JOB OF CLEARING THE DECKS OF USED SHELL CASINGS, AIRCRAFT WRECKAGE...

...AND BODY PARTS.

AT SUNSET, GENERAL QUARTERS WAS SOUNDED AGAIN.

EVEN THOUGH THE JAPANESE NO LONGER RULED THE SEAS, THE SAILORS WOULD GET LITTLE SLEEP UNTIL ALL THE ENEMY AIR BASES IN THE PHILIPPINES HAD BEEN NEUTRALIZED.

THE END

Marion "Frank" Walker
Capturing Mount Suribachi
—The Battle of Iwo Jima
February 19, 1945

FEBRUARY 19, 1945, 0650 HOURS, ON THE DECK OF THE USS MISSOULA.

PREPARE TO BOARD YOUR LANDING CRAFT!

HUH?

THE LOUDSPEAKER ANNOUNCEMENT SNAPPED 19-YEAR-OLD CORPORAL FRANK WALKER OUT OF HIS THOUGHTS OF HOME.

HE DESCENDED THE JACOB'S LADDER TO ONE OF THE LANDING CRAFT, OR HIGGINS BOATS, THAT WOULD TAKE THE MEN OF THE 5TH MARINES DIVISION ONTO THE BEACH AT IWO JIMA.

TWO HOURS LATER, WALKER'S HIGGINS BOAT PEELED OFF FROM A LARGE GROUP OF CIRCLING VEHICLES. HE WAS PART OF THE SECOND WAVE.

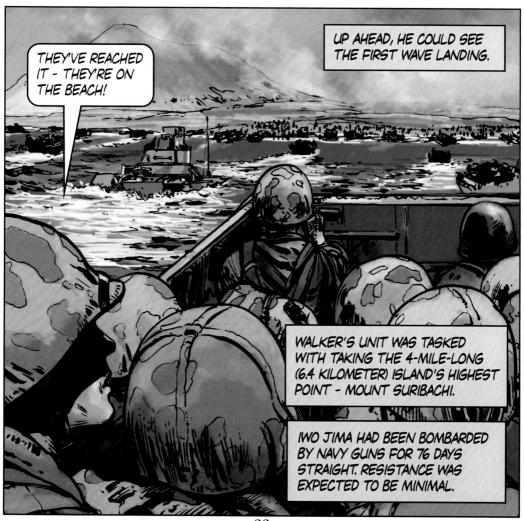

UP AHEAD, HE COULD SEE THE FIRST WAVE LANDING.

THEY'VE REACHED IT - THEY'RE ON THE BEACH!

WALKER'S UNIT WAS TASKED WITH TAKING THE 4-MILE-LONG (6.4 KILOMETER) ISLAND'S HIGHEST POINT - MOUNT SURIBACHI.

IWO JIMA HAD BEEN BOMBARDED BY NAVY GUNS FOR 76 DAYS STRAIGHT. RESISTANCE WAS EXPECTED TO BE MINIMAL.

EXPLOSIONS FROM MORTAR ROUNDS SUDDENLY RIPPED THE AIR, AS THE FIRST WAVE MOVED UP THE BEACH.

BOOM! KERRACK!

AMONG THE OTHER ARTILLERY THE JAPANESE HAD PLACED AROUND SURIBACHI WERE ENORMOUS SPIGOT MORTARS.

FOOOM!

KAROOM!

A SPIGOT MORTAR ROUND CAME SCREAMING IN SIDEWAYS AND EXPLODED AT THE FRONT OF WALKER'S BOAT, TEARING THE GATE OFF.

THE SURVIVORS HAD SECONDS TO GET OUT AS THE BOAT CAPSIZED.

THE SHORELINE WAS LITTERED WITH DEAD AND DYING MARINES FROM THE FIRST WAVE. WALKER TRIED DESPERATELY TO DIG A FOXHOLE TO SHELTER FROM THE MORTARS.

THIS SAND - IT JUST CAVES BACK IN ON ITSELF.

BOOOM!

A SHORT DISTANCE ABOVE THE MARINES TRYING TO WORK THEIR WAY UP THE TERRACES, ARTILLERY GUNS FIRED RANDOMLY TOWARD THE HILL.

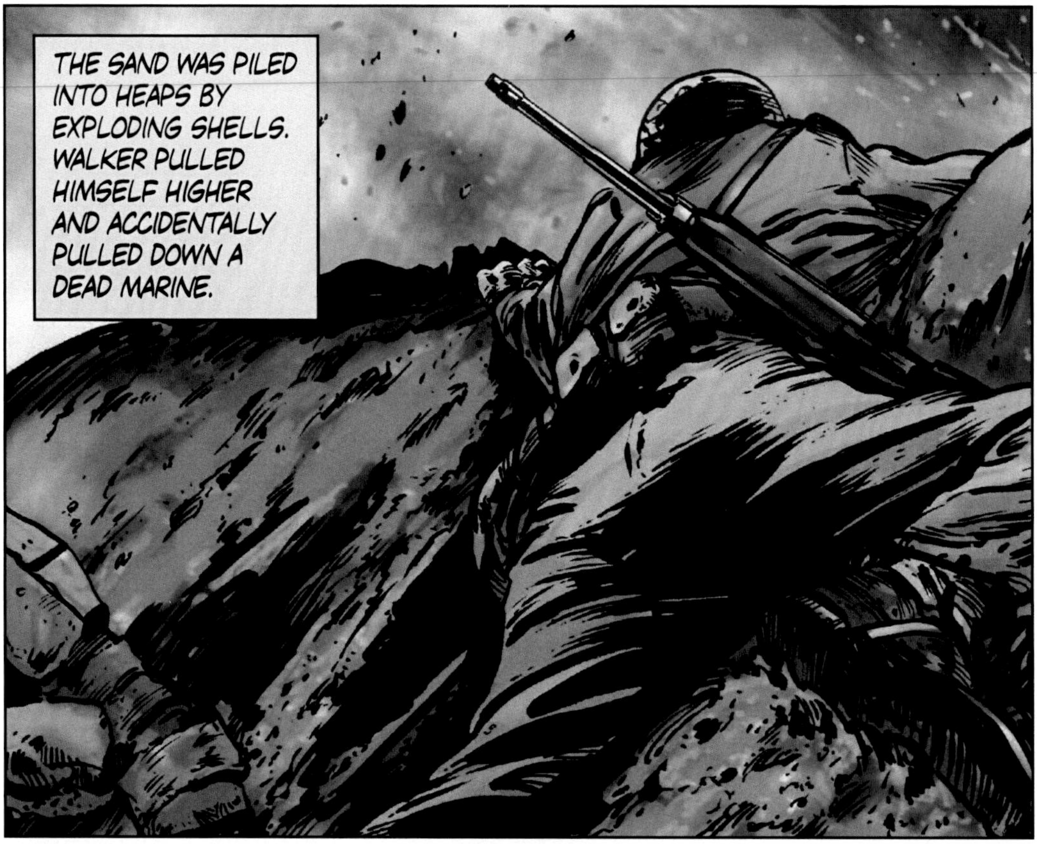
THE SAND WAS PILED INTO HEAPS BY EXPLODING SHELLS. WALKER PULLED HIMSELF HIGHER AND ACCIDENTALLY PULLED DOWN A DEAD MARINE.

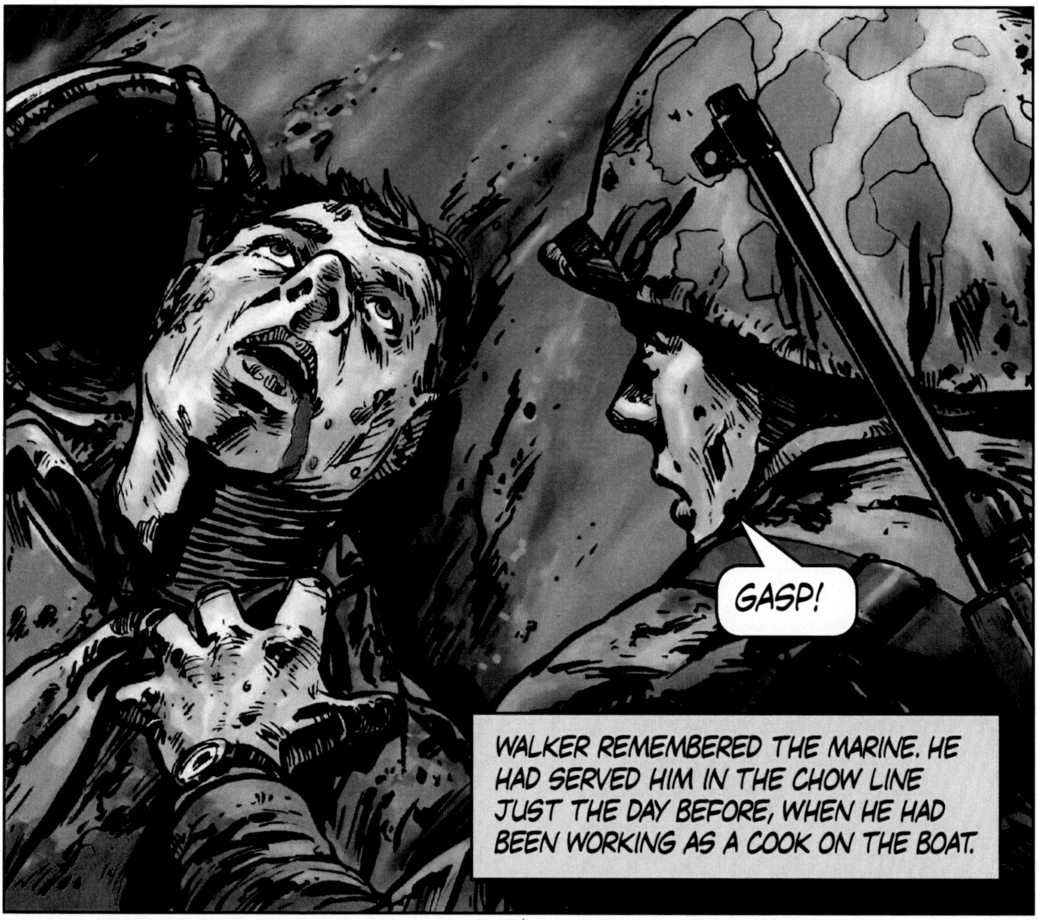
GASP!
WALKER REMEMBERED THE MARINE. HE HAD SERVED HIM IN THE CHOW LINE JUST THE DAY BEFORE, WHEN HE HAD BEEN WORKING AS A COOK ON THE BOAT.

THIS BEACH - IT'S JUST A KILLING FIELD.

THE BLACK VOLCANIC SAND WAS STAINED PURPLE WITH THE BLOOD OF MARINES.

MORE AND MORE TROOPS WERE SLOWLY PUSHED ONTO THE BEACH*.

AFTER TWO DAYS, THE FOOTHILL OF MOUNT SURIBACHI WAS FINALLY REACHED.

*30,000 MARINES WERE LANDED IN TOTAL.

THE JAPANESE WERE DUG INTO HIDDEN POSITIONS ALL OVER THE FOOTHILL. A MARINE CARRYING A FLAME THROWER STEPPED FORWARD.

IT'S NO GOOD – IT DOESN'T WORK.

GRIT FROM THE BEACH HAD JAMMED THE MECHANISM.

BUT SOON...

WOOOOOOSH!

ALL THE JAPANESE POSITIONS WOULD HAVE TO BE CLEARED BEFORE THEY COULD REACH THE SUMMIT.

FEBRUARY 23, WALKER STOOD STARING INTO THE CRATER OF MOUNT SURIBACHI. HE WAS ONE OF ABOUT 45 MEN WHO HAD MADE IT TO THE TOP.

A TRAIL OF WOUNDED, DEAD, AND DYING MARINES LED ALL THE WAY BACK DOWN TO THE BEACH.

LATER WALKER LOOKED ON AS THE FAMOUS SECOND FLAG WAS RAISED.

THEY HAD THE HEIGHTS. NOW THEIR COMMANDERS HOPED TO GAIN THE REST OF IWO JIMA QUICKLY.

BUT AS HE LOOKED TOWARD THE NORTH OF THE ISLAND, TO WHERE FOURTH DIVISION WAS BATTLING TO SECURE AN AIRFIELD, WALKER WONDERED...

WE'VE SUFFERED SO MANY LOSSES TO GET THIS LITTLE DISTANCE...

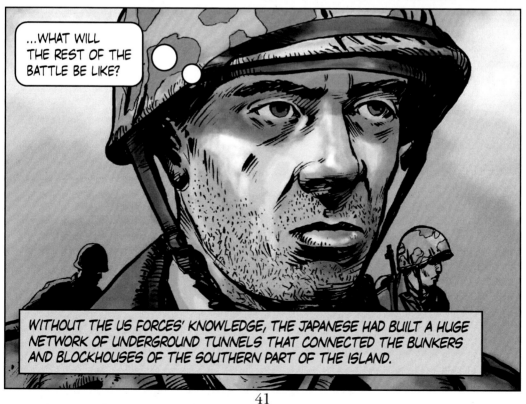

...WHAT WILL THE REST OF THE BATTLE BE LIKE?

WITHOUT THE US FORCES' KNOWLEDGE, THE JAPANESE HAD BUILT A HUGE NETWORK OF UNDERGROUND TUNNELS THAT CONNECTED THE BUNKERS AND BLOCKHOUSES OF THE SOUTHERN PART OF THE ISLAND.

IN ALL OF JAPAN'S HISTORY, NO FOREIGN ARMY HAD EVER SUCCESSFULLY INVADED. THE 22,630 DEFENDING SOLDIERS HAD VOWED TO KILL 10 AMERICANS EACH BEFORE THEY THEMSELVES WERE KILLED.

EVERY TIME A BUNKER WAS CLEARED, DEFENDERS WOULD SNEAK BACK IN AND AMBUSH ADVANCING MARINES. THE POSITIONS HAD TO BE RETAKEN MANY TIMES OVER, AT HUGE COST.

IT TOOK 34 MORE DAYS OF CONTINUAL FIGHTING TO SECURE THE ISLAND. MORE THAN 26,000 MARINES WERE KILLED OR WOUNDED - THE BIGGEST SACRIFICE IN THE 170-YEAR HISTORY OF THE UNITED STATES MARINE CORPS.

THE END

ULTIMATE FORCE

During the Battle of Okinawa (April 1 to June 22, 1945), US forces suffered 62,000 casualties with more than 12,000 killed or missing. Of the more than 100,000 Japanese defenders, only about 7,400 were captured alive. In addition to this, there were 142,058 civilian casualties. Okinawa was by far the bloodiest battle in the whole Pacific War.

DECISION POINT

The Battle of Iwo Jima had resulted in an almost one-for-one casualty rate. Military analysts estimated that an invasion of the Japanese home island would cost more than 500,000 combined military and civilian casualties in the early stages alone.

American troops in Okinawa listen to a radio report of Germany's surrender on May 8, 1945.

Since February 1945, wave after wave of B-29 Superfortresses had dropped firebombs on key Japanese cities to stop war production and break the Japanese's will to fight. The secret atom bomb had originally been developed in a race to beat the Germans from developing it first. On May 8, 1945, Germany had finally surrendered. On May 10, a meeting was held to discuss possible Japanese targets for the bomb.

On July 26, an ultimatum was issued demanding the complete surrender of Japan or they would suffer *"...the inevitable and complete destruction of the Japanese armed forces and just as inevitably the utter devastation of the Japanese homeland."* Japan ignored the ultimatum and President Harry Truman authorized use of the bomb.

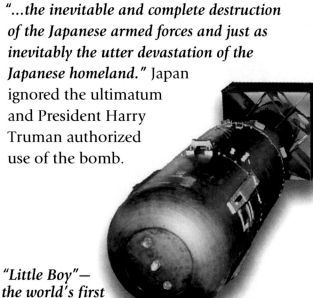

More than 100,000 Japanese people and much of Tokyo was destroyed in a firestorm caused by raids between March 9–10, 1945.

"Little Boy"— the world's first nuclear bomb

ZERO HOUR

The cities chosen had been spared from the nightly bombing raids. To the Americans, it was important to demonstrate the full potential of their nuclear weapon to shock Japan into unconditional surrender.

On August 6, at 0830 hours, under clear skies, the B-29 Enola Gay released the atomic bomb "Little Boy" over the center of Hiroshima, in southern Japan. It took 45 seconds to fall before it exploded and changed the world forever.

In Hiroshima, everything within a 1-mile (1.6 km) radius of ground zero was flattened. Seventy thousand people were killed instantly. Thousands more died later of burns and radiation poisoning.

A second bomb (right) was dropped on Nagasaki on August 9.

The industrial valley of Nagasaki lay in ruins.

The two bombs, combined with the Soviet invasion of Japanese-occupied Manchuria, left Japan reeling. They had hoped the Russians would broker a favorable peace for them. Japan surrendered unconditionally on September 2, 1945.

GLOSSARY

Allies The joint military forces fighting against Germany and Japan during World War II

ambush A sudden attack combined with the element of surprise

ammunition Objects, such as bullets, that can be fired from guns

artillery High-caliber weapons used by crews during battle

bombarded Continuously attacked with bombs and other such weapons by an enemy

carnage A large number of deaths

casualties Those in hostile engagements that die, are captured or go missing

conquer To bring an area under one's control by force

decimated To destroy a large number of things from a group

divine God-like or coming from a god

doomsday The day when everything comes to an end

fascist One adhering to dictatorial control

flak Bursting shells used by anti-aircraft artillery

ground zero The exact center of the site of a nuclear explosion

The destroyer USS Shaw explodes at Oahu Island, Pearl Harbor, Hawaii, 1941

infamy Fame brought on by evil or criminal workings

infirmary A place of medical treatment

kamikaze World War II Japanese pilots trained for suicide missions

lumbering To act with slow and heavy movements

neutralized The destruction of a threat

port The left-hand side of a ship

recall A given order to return

sanctions Penalties brought about through pressure, about to assure the desired actions

scouting The act of going ahead of a troop to inspect an area in secret

severing The separation of a once-singular object into two

squadron A unit in the air force consisting of two or more flights

starboard The right-hand side of a ship

stern The rear of a ship

turret A low, heavily armored structure on a warship, that is equipped with guns and is run by a crew

veteran One who has worked in a specific area for a long enough time to gain significant experience

Zero A type of Japanese aircraft

Marines fight on the Japanese island of Okinawa, 1945

INDEX

A

Allies 4–7
ambush 6, 42
ammunition 15, 26
artillery 34, 36
atomic bomb 44–45
Australia 5

B

B-29 44–45
Banzai Charge 27
Battle of Leyte Gulf
   7, 20
Battle of Midway
   5–6, 8, 19
Battle of Okinawa
   44, 47

C

casualties 30, 44
China 4–5
code 6
Coral Sea 5–6

D

Doolittle Raid 5
doomsday 7

E

Enola Gay 45

F

fascist 4
Fahey, James J. 20–31
firebombs 44
flak 12

G

Gay, George 8–19
Germany 4, 44
ground zero 45
Guadalcanal 6
Guam 5, 7

H

Hawaii 4–6, 46
Hirohito, Emperor 7
Hiroshima 45

I

infirmary 30
Italy 4
Iwo Jima 7, 32–33, 40, 44

K

Kaga 12, 14
kamikaze 7, 20, 27, 29

L

"Little Boy" 44–45

M

Mount Suribachi 32–34,
   38, 40

N

Nagasaki 45
Nimitz, Chester 6

O

Okinawa 7, 44, 47

P

Pearl Harbor 4–5, 46
Philippines 5, 7, 20, 31

R

Roosevelt, Franklin D. 4

S

sanctions 4
scouting 8
Special Attack Corps 27
squadron 8, 10, 19

T

Torpedo Bombers, 8
   12, 16
Truman, Harry 44
turret 25

U

USS *Arizona* 4
USS *Hornet* 8
USS *Lexington* 5
USS *Missoula* 32
USS *Montpelier* 20, 26
USS *Yorktown* 5, 6

V

veteran 6

W

Wake Island 5
Walker, Marion "Frank"
   32–43

Y

Yamamoto, Admiral 6
Yamoto 6

Z

Zeros 9, 11, 16